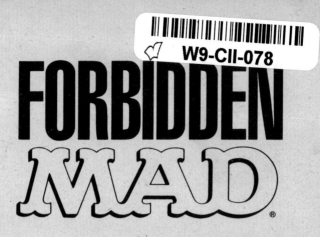

FORBIDDEN
MAD®

Edited by
Albert B. Feldstein

WARNER BOOKS

A Warner Communications Company

Warner Books, Inc.
666 Fifth Avenue
New York, N.Y. 10103

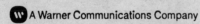 A Warner Communications Company

Printed in the United States of America

First Printing: October, 1984

10 9 8 7 6 5 4 3 2 1

IN A GALAXY MILLIONS OF LIGHT YEARS AWAY A BAD EVIL GALACTIC EMPIRE HAS BUILT A SUPER SPACE STATION THAT CAN DESTROY AN ENTIRE PLANET, LED BY GOOD PRINCESS LAIDUP, REBEL FORCES STEAL THE PLANS...AND A MIGHTY PLANS...AND A MIGHTY STAR WAR TAKES PLACE!!!

That rotten, evil Galactic Empire . . . killing and **destroying** everything in sight!!

Wiping out planets and civilization, I can almost excuse! But when they start picking on poor defenseless movie introductions . . .

Incredible! Our ship goes faster than the speed of light, and our guns fire almost as fast as the speed of light!
Yeah . . . so guess what just happened! We shot ourselves down!!
What?! You mean to tell me that the In-Flight Movie is Bugs Bunny chasing the Roadrunner up a hill?!?
What do you expect on a seven second flight . . . "The Godfather"?
How high up into space would you say this ship goes?
Quiet! I'm about to say a prayer before we go into battle . . .
OUR FATHER WHO ART BELOW US IN HEAVEN—
That high, huh?
Boy, these space ships are noisy!! Maybe that's why they call this movie . . .
STAR ROARS
ARTIST: HARRY NORTH, ESQ.
WRITER: LARRY SIEGEL WITH DICK DE BARTOLO

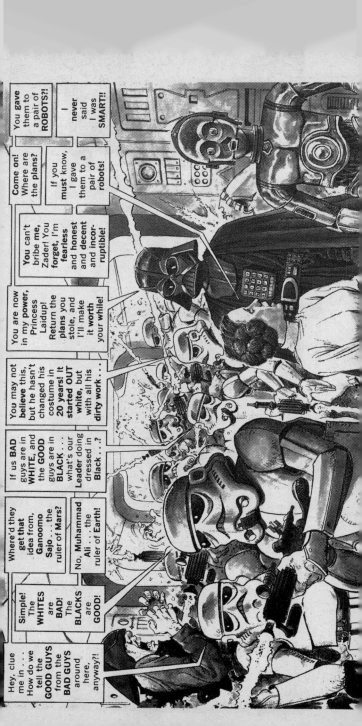

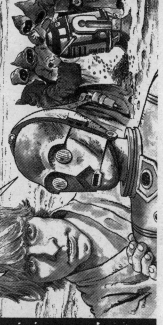

Hi, strangers! I'm **Lube Skystalker!** I'm a senior at **Buffooin Tech,** where I major in *Incredible Space Heroics!*

Gracious, there **couldn't** be any money in **THAT** field!

You're telling me! That's why I'm minoring in **Space Accounting!** Hey, anyone ever tell you you look like an **"Oscar"?!?**

Take a good look! With your performance in this film, it's as close as you'll ever get to an Academy Award!

Bar-Stool, we seem to be lost! Oh, dear... look what's coming! **Fiendish creatures** about to tear us limb from limb and commit **unspeakable acts of cruelty upon us...!**

Follow the yellow sand road! Follow the yellow sand road! Follow... follow ...follow ...follow ... Follow the yellow sand road!

Beep! Zit! Gack!

TRANSLATION: And then again ...there's an outside chance they may be **Space Munchkins!**

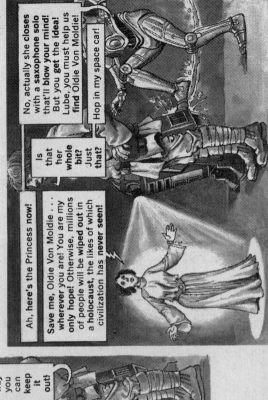

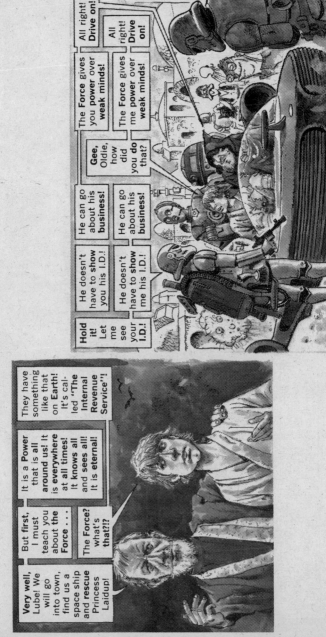

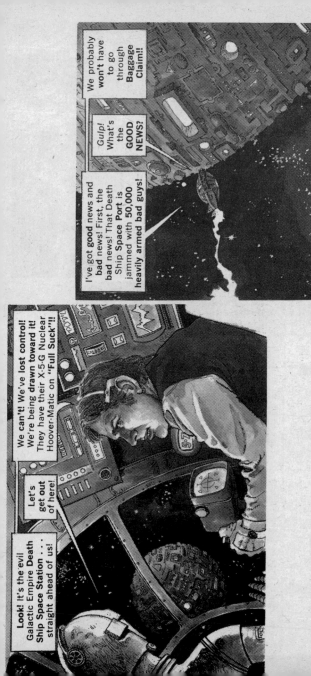

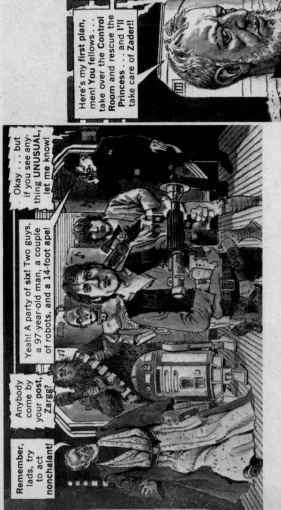

So, Zader! We meet again! Prepare your Light Ray Sword for a duel to the death! I shall triumph because I have The Force!
Get ready to die, you black-hearted villain!!
Good lord! My light ray has gone out!!
How ironic! Betrayed by a lack of faith in The Force . . .
. . . and a ridiculously short . . . gasp . . . extension cord!

EARLY ONE EVENING IN ATLANTIC CITY

THE
LIGHTER
SIDE OF...

DAN

GER

ARTIST & WRITER: DAVE BERG

Oh, Daddy!! WAAAA!!

Honey . . . what happened to you?

I—sob-sob—I—I failed my—sob—driving test!!

Oh, you poor, poor little darling . . .

And I **know** how much you wanted to **pass,** too! What a **tragedy** for you! We can **talk** about it later! Right now, why don't you go to your room, **close the door** and have a good cry! Get it all out of your system!

Sob . . . sob . . .

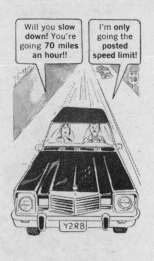

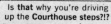

We got **one** guy in my dorm who **actually believes** in **Witchcraft** and **Voodoo** and **Black Magic** and like that!

Can you **imagine?** In **this** place of higher learning . . . in **this** the atomic age . . . when we've put **men** on the **moon** . . . there is **still** one jerk who **believes** in ridiculous, superstitions mumbo-jumbo **nonsense** like that!

I guess you **really told him off,** eh!

Are you **crazy?!**

He's **liable** to put some kind of **CURSE** on me!!

There are guys with **macho** . . . like a **Fireman!** He's got a **dangerous job!** And a **Police-man's** job is no piece of cake!

And a **Skyscraper Window Washer** has a dangerous job! So does a **Lion Tamer** and a **Professional Athlete** and a **Construction Worker** and a **Space Astronaut!** They **all** have dangerous jobs!

And what am I?! A lousy **HIGH SCHOOL TEACHER?**

THE MOST DANGEROUS JOB OF ALL!

Gambling is stupid! "No," you say? You wanna bet?! Okay, go ahead and gamble . . . but know the odds. Because knowing the odds is necessary if you're gonna gamble and win. And that means not only the odds on horse races and ballgames, but on life's everyday situations as well. To help you in this important area, here is . . .

THE
MAD

IT'S 3 TO 1 . . .

**. . . when you get stuck in traffic,
you'll have to go to the bathroom.**

IT'S 7 TO 5...

. . . you'll get a whole new cluster of
pimples the day of the Senior Prom.

BOOK OF ODDS

ARTIST: PAUL COKER, JR.   WRITER: STAN HART

IT'S 2 TO 1...

... your nose will start to run when you don't have a handkerchief.

IT'S 5 TO 1...

... that when you get a Summer job, your Mother will come into the store every day to see how you're doing.

... that the morning you have an important job interview, your alarm will fail to go off.

... you'll finish an exam in record time, only to find out later that there were 13 questions on the last page you didn't see.

IT'S 4 TO 3...

... your finger will slip just
as you dial the last number of
a long distance telephone call.

IT'S 5 TO 3...

... on the first day of your family vacation, your Mother and Father will have an
argument, and then fight the entire trip.

IT'S 3 TO 1...

. . . that the next time you have a
blind date, you'll be disappointed.

AND IT'S EVEN MONEY...

. . . your date will be disappointed.

. . . when you're selected to lead the assembly in "The Pledge Of Allegiance" you'll discover later your fly was open.

. . . it'll rain on your overnight hike.

... while trying to impress your pretty tennis partner, you'll hit her in the back of her head with your first serve.

... whenever you try to hail a cab to impress your date, you'll have ugly sweat stains under your arms.

IT'S 4 TO 1 . . .

. . . your Mother will take a "terribly important" telephone message for you but she can't remember who it's from.

IT'S 4 TO 3 . . .

. . . your date's old man is asleep when you go out, but awake when you return.

. . . the worst picture ever taken of you will be in your School Year Book.

. . . when you go to the bathroom in your date's house, the toilet doesn't work.

TEN

LITTLE

Each one in his glory,
Sold their wares in stores like these
Until...well, here's their story—

BUSINESSMEN

ARTIST: HARRY NORTH, ESQ.

WRITER: FRANK JACOBS

IDEA: CHARLES M. De FUCCIO

Ten Little Businessmen,
Making out just fine;
One clashed with a fast food chain;
The crunch left only nine.

Nine Little Businessmen,
Pondering their fate;
One defied a labor boss;
The strike left only eight.

Eight Little Businessmen,
With no hope in Heaven;
One received a raise in rent;
The squeeze left only seven.

Seven Little Businessmen,
In a dreadful fix;
One "protection" wouldn't pay;
The hit left only six.

Six Little Businessmen,
Only half alive;
One was burgled in the night;
The haul left only five.

Five Little Businessmen,
In a losing war;
One laughed off a junkie's threat;
The shot left only four.

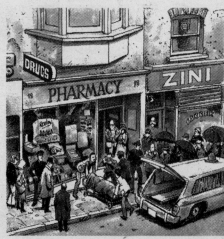

Four Little Businessmen,
Watching crime run free;
One had his insurance dropped;
The shock left only three.

Three Little Businessmen,
Praying they'll pull through;
One was stormed by looting mobs;
The loss left only two.

Two Little Businessmen,
Bankrupt and undone;
One employed "Tyrone the Torch;"
The blaze left only one.

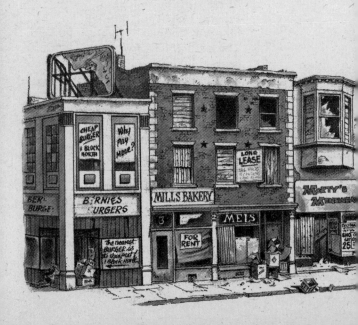

One Little Businessman,
Scared and on the run;
He's closing up for good today;
And then there will be none.

BEFORE THE ROCK CONCERT

WRITER & ARTIST: SERGIO ARAGONES

Recently, there has been an alarming upsurge of **weird behavior** among a group of our young people! We mean **real funky stuff**, like **being polite** and getting **short haircuts** and wearing **clean, neat clothes**! Naturally the **parents** of these youngsters are **worried**! And so, as a public service, MAD now investigates the man who is **responsible** for this freaky behavior, the head of **The Loonatication Church**, the Reverend Sun Set Loony, who has been named...

MAD'S "RELIGIOUS CULT LEADER" OF THE YEAR

Reverend Loony ...I'm Mike Malice ...for MAD Magazine! They've asked me to conduct an "In-Depth Interview" with you, so—

Say, this is some fantastic place you have here! What do you call it... SAN SIMEON EAST??

I call it "THE GARDEN OF EDEN"! Would you care for an apple?

No, thanks! Y'know... I always thought that Religious Leaders lived—er— SIMPLY!

You thought wrong! Why shouldn't I live as comfortably as a Rock Star or a crooked **ex-President**? Do you know that it is written: "The New Messiah shall come from **Korea** ... he shall be **five-foot-two-inches tall** ... have dark hair and eyes ... and be born under the sign of **Taurus The Bull** ..." which happens to be **MY SIGN!?!**

No, where is that written?

In my book, "THE WIT AND WISDOM OF REVEREND LOONY, THE NEW MESSIAH"!

ARTIST: GEORGE WOODBRIDGE   WRITER: LOU SILVERSTONE

You haven't read my book?! It usually sells for $5.95, but we're having a SPECIAL SALE this week! For $5.95, you get my book PLUS this Volume of Authentic Golden Oldie Korean Hymns —including such favorites as "Let's All Gather At The Bank Vault"...PLUS "The Korean CIA Handbook On How To Buy Friends And Influence People"...AND this real collectors' item, the "Reverend Loony Superstar Tee Shirt"!!

Reverend Loony...if you ever decide to leave the Religion Business, you have a great future on Madison Avenue...!

Tell, me, sir! Why did you come to the U.S.?

I was in my garden one day when I received a message!

A Divine Message from God?

No, it was a Mailgram from my Accountant! He explained that "Religious Organizations" do not have to pay TAXES in the U.S.! So I packed my carpetbag and here I am! And it's a good thing I CAME to your country!

Why? Because there are so many Americans who need salvation?

No, because there are so many dumb suckers who are willing to pay $2.00 for a box of lousy candy that costs me 23 cents!

KEEP AMERICA BEAUTIFUL CANDY

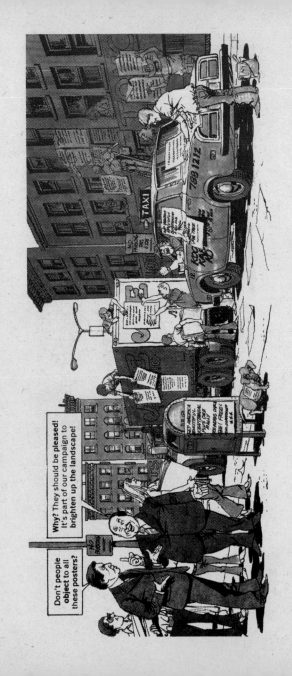

ONE SATURDAY AFTERNOON

YOU'RE AN OPTIMIST

YOU'RE AN ETERNAL OPTIMIST IF . . .

. . . you assume that you'll get your flat tire changed in a jiffy, now that a whole motorcycle gang has stopped to lend you a helping hand.

ARTIST: JACK DAVIS   WRITER: TOM KOCH WITH JACK KENT

re constantly in fear of being exposed as complete
diots. But actually, you're giving your secret away
y stupid optimism you don't even know you're exhibit-
ng. So there isn't a moment to lose in comparing your
wn behavior with these MAD examples. Because if you
isplay any of these symptoms, it's a sure sign that—

ETERNAL
F...

YOU'RE AN ETERNAL OPTIMIST IF . . .

. . . you scan the movie ads, expecting to
find something to take the whole family to.

YOU'RE AN ETERNAL OPTIMIST IF . . .

. . . you can't imagine why your Doctor would call in four Specialists for consultation, unless he needs their help to tell you how well you're progressing.

YOU'RE AN ETERNAL OPTIMIST IF . . .

. . . you think you've found a garage sale where a millionaire art collector is disposing of genuine art masterpieces at five bucks apiece.

YOU'RE AN ETERNAL OPTIMIST IF...

...you can hardly wait for some newly-elected politician to take office so he can start keeping his campaign promises.

YOU'RE AN ETERNAL OPTIMIST IF...

. . . you ask your Dentist if it's going to hurt, and he says, "No!" . . . and you really believe him.

YOU'RE AN ETERNAL OPTIMIST IF . . .

...you assume there's nothing to hang-gliding
that you can't teach yourself as you go along.

YOU'RE AN ETERNAL OPTIMIST IF . . .

. . . you figure that arriving at the airport ten minutes late is
close enough because they'll hold the plane until you get there.

YOU'RE AN ETERNAL OPTIMIST IF . . .

. . . you think your new after-shave lotion will make women find you irresistible when they never even found you tolerable before.

YOU'RE AN ETERNAL OPTIMIST IF . . .

. . . you expect anything you order from a mail order house to look even half as good as the picture in the catalogue.

YOU'RE AN ETERNAL OPTIMIST IF . . .

. . . being allowed to suit up for Junior College football prompts you to start planning your illustrious career in the N.F.L.

YOU'RE AN ETERNAL OPTIMIST IF . . .

. . . you have complete faith in those old adages that barking dogs never bite . . . and bees never sting if you just leave them alone . . . and lightning never strikes twice in the same place.

YOU'RE AN ETERNAL OPTIMIST IF . . .

. . . you assume every girl you've ever dated is free tonight, and just waiting by the phone in hopes you'll call.

YOU'RE AN ETERNAL OPTIMIST IF . . .

. . . you buy a catalogue that describes valuable coins on the assumption that your pocket change is worth a fortune.

YOU'RE AN ETERNAL OPTIMIST IF . . .

. . . you assume you'll be able to see and hear everything perfectly from the $2.00 seats at a Neil Diamond concert.

YOU'RE AN ETERNAL OPTIMIST IF . . .

. . . you think that, even though your gas gauge reads empty, you have enough to make it to the next station.

YOU'RE AN ETERNAL OPTIMIST IF . . .

. . . you decide to wait for the next bus
because this one is already too crowded.

YOU'RE AN ETERNAL OPTIMIST IF . . .

. . . you really expect the other
driver to yield the right of way.

YOU'RE AN ETERNAL OPTIMIST IF . . .

. . . you buy a "new, improved" product
and expect it to be new and improved.

YOU'RE AN ETERNAL OPTIMIST IF . . .

...you take your kids to the zoo...thinking that you're finally getting them away from all that sex and violence.

YOU'RE AN ETERNAL OPTIMIST IF . . .

. . . you expect to look like the model looked when you buy the dress in your size that she just wore.

YOU'RE AN ETERNAL OPTIMIST IF . . .

. . . you expect your new 1978 car to perform as
well as that old Studebaker you're trading in.

YOU'RE AN ETERNAL OPTIMIST IF . . .

. . . you don't foresee any problems in hitchhiking around the world
because you're sure that all foreigners love American tourists.

A MAD LOOK AT... SOME LEGENDARY COMMODES

JESSE JAMES'

ARTIST: PAUL COKER, JR.
WRITER: PAUL PETER PORGES

DRACULA'S

KING TUT'S

LITTLE JACK HORNER'S

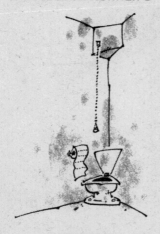

DADDY LONG LEGS'

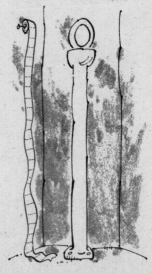

HOUDINI'S

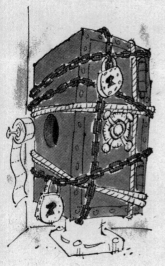

CASANOVA'S

RONALD McDONALD'S

ROBIN HOOD'S

KING ARTHUR'S
(AND HIS KNIGHTS')

LOUIS XIV'S

SUPERMAN'S

ROBINSON CRUSOE'S
(AND HIS MAN, FRIDAY'S)

THE THREE BEARS'

THE MARQUIS DE SADE'S
(GUEST BATHROOM)

This next article deals with the incredible growth of Crime in our country. We had originally planned to present an incisive, objective introduction to this story . . . but unfortunately, our "Introduction Writer" was mugged on the way to the office. So lacking it, here's

A MAD LOOK AT

THE CHANGING FACE OF CRIME

ARTIST: JACK DAVIS   WRITER: LARRY SIEGEL

REMEMBER WHEN...

. . . "the punishment fit the crime", and a guy who committed anything from a misdemeanor to murder pretty much got the sentence he deserved.

TODAY...

. . . a guy who rips off a bank, pistol-whips a teller and drives away with 9 hostages gets a "suspended sentence" because it's only his first offense.

REMEMBER WHEN...

. . . they used to protect young people from possible homosexual assaults by throwing all the "gays" into jails.

TODAY...

. . . they want to take young people *out* of jails to protect them from homosexual assaults by the "gays" who are *in.*

REMEMBER WHEN...

...a notorious criminal invariably ended up being grilled in court... found guilty... and forced to pay the price for his terrible crimes.

TODAY...

...he's interviewed on television, and writes books, and the price for his terrible crimes runs into millions of dollars. Only *they* pay *him*!

REMEMBER WHEN...

... you could always spot crooks. They looked tough ... wore caps, eye-masks and turtleneck sweaters ... and said things like, "Hands up, youse guys!"

TODAY...

... most crooks look like oil tycoons ... dress like bankers ... and talk like politicians. Mainly because they *ARE* oil tycoons, bankers and politicians.

REMEMBER WHEN...

. . . a convicted murderer usually got a death sentence, which meant he had a choice of the electric chair . . . or the gallows . . . or the gas chamber.

TODAY...

. . . he gets "life," which means he's out in 7 years, which means he has a choice of killing you before or after his first visit to his parole officer.

REMEMBER WHEN...

... it was rare that a person was mugged and knifed on the street... and when it did happen, 14 people would run over and help the victim.

TODAY...

... 15 lawyers and the American Civil Liberties Union run over to help the *mugger*, and Ralph Nader accuses American industry of making lousy knives.

REMEMBER WHEN...

. . . a convicted criminal, like maybe
an embezzler, spent years in jail . . .
and all he had waiting for him when he
got out was a new suit and 20 bucks.

TODAY...

. . . an embezzler is fined $30,000 for
his crime . . . and all he has waiting
for him when he gets out is $470,000
out of the half million bucks he stole.

REMEMBER WHEN...

... the corner cop was a servant of all of the people... who earned our respect by standing with his hand like this ...

TODAY...

... he's a defender of special people ... who has lost our respect, because he stands with his hand like this ...

REMEMBER WHEN...

... you used to get 48 pages of MAD for 25¢, which you considered to be a rip-off, and thought that the publisher was a crook.

TODAY...

... you get the same 48 pages for 60¢ ... and the crook publisher considers himself to be a great environmentalist for recycling garbage as entertainment.

A MAD
SUN 'N'

LOOK AT SURF

WRITER AND ARTIST:
PAUL PETER PORGES

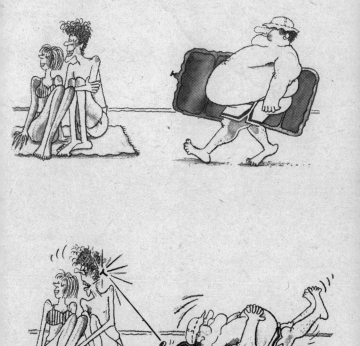

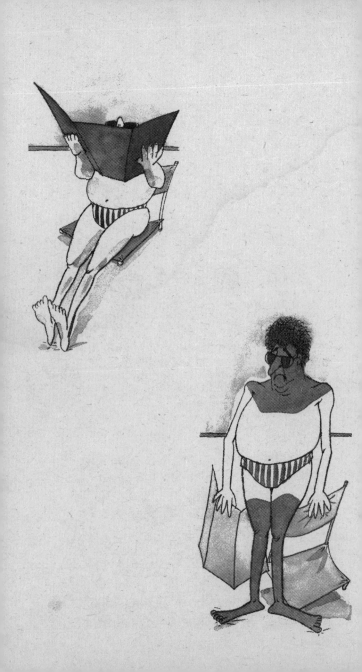

INVEN
WE'D LIKE

FOR TAILGATERS WITH BRIGHT HEADLIGHTS ON . . .

TIONS
TO SEE

ARTIST: AL JAFFEE   WRITER: PAUL PETER PORGES

REAR-MOUNTED BRIGHT LIGHTS

FOR MESSY ROOMS THAT NEED QUICK CLEANINGS . . .

INSTANT-NEAT SCREENS

FOR THAT HARD-TO-READ SMALL PRINT...

STRETCHABLE PAPER

FOR THOSE LIP-AND-TONGUE-SCALDING BEVERAGES . . .

THERMOMETER WARNING SPOONS

FOR PEOPLE WHO FORGET GALOSHES IN WET WEATHER . . .

BUILT-IN PUDDLE CROSSERS

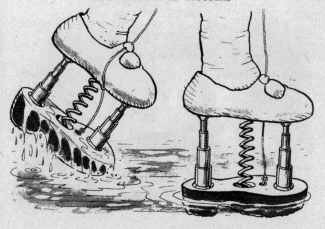

FOR MONOPOLIZED PUBLIC TELEPHONE BOOTHS . . .

THREE-MINUTE TIMED EJECTORS

FOR THOSE ELUSIVE, DISAPPEARING TUBE TOPS . . .

TOOTHPASTE TUBE TOP GUARDS

FOR PEOPLE WHO HATE HAVING THEIR FOOD TASTED . . .

SAMPLE-PROOF PLATES

FOR PROTECTION AGAINST SELF-SLAMMING DOORS . . .

EXTENDING THIRD-ARM DOOR-HOLDERS

FOR PEOPLE CURSED WITH NOISY SLEEP MATES . . .

SOUND-PROOF ISOLATION BELLS

FOR CROWDED AIRLINE BAGGAGE PICK-UP AREAS . . .

REMOTE-CONTROLLED LUGGAGE-IDENTIFIERS

FOR ACCIDENT-PRONE BATHERS . . .

SLIP-PROOF SAFETY HARNESSES WITH OVERHEAD TRACKS

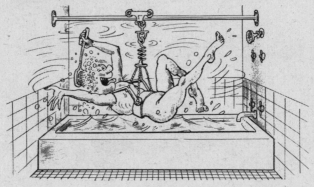

FOR CHRONIC UMBRELLA-MISPLACERS . . .

PERSONAL PORT-A-BRELLA SCABBARDS

THE
LIGHTER
SIDE OF...

GAD

GETS

WRITER & ARTIST: DAVID BERG

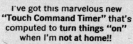

I've got this marvelous new "Touch Command Timer" that's computed to **turn things "on"** when I'm **not at home**!!

It turns on the **lights** . . . it turns on the **water sprinkler** . . . it turns on the **radio** . . .

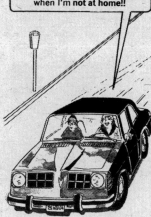

It even turns on the **electric oven** and **starts dinner** while I'm away!

If it **does** all that . . . **why** are you **rushing home?**

I forgot to turn it on!!

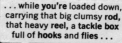

Arnold, baby, you look like you've got the weight of the **whole world** on your shoulders! Why the **hangdog expression?** What's **eating you**, anyway?

I've got **troubles!** **Big** troubles! I'm **terribly worried** about my Wife!!

Your **WIFE!?** Oh, my Lord!!

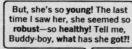

But, she's so **young!** The last time I saw her, she seemed so **robust**—so **healthy!** Tell me, Buddy-boy, **what** has she got?!

My brand new $14,000 car!

Sir, I've got a letter from a woman who says she bought one of our appliances back in **1952**! She says she's **still** using it today! What's more, it has never needed a **single repair**!

That's **remarkable**!

I want you to **write** to that woman and offer her five hun—... no, make that a **thousand dollars** for that appliance!

Yes, sir...

And when you get it, have Engineering **strip it down** and **examine it thoroughly**! Have them **find out** exactly what made it **last** so long!

Yes, sir! It could **revolutionize** the **whole** industry!

Right! And we **don't** want to make that **same** mistake again!

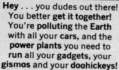

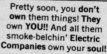

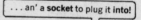

What the heck is THAT thing?!?

That's my Telephone Answering Machine!

It cost a fortune . . . and I had to stall paying other bills so I could buy it . . . but it was worth it! While I'm out, this crazy machine records all my incoming telephone messages!

Gee, how does it work?

I'll show you! All I do is re-wind the cassette like this . . . then push the "play" button like this . . . and listen to the calls I got!

This is the Telephone Company! Because of non-payment of your telephone bill, as of tomorrow, we are disconnecting your phone!

ONE EVENING

IN A

BUS

STATION

WE'RE ALL FAMILIAR WITH THE "STROKE" HANDICAPS IN GOLF AND THE "WEIGHT" HANDICAPS IN HORSERACING. ACCORDING TO THE DICTIONARY, A "HANDICAP" IS A DISADVANTAGE OR ADVANTAGE PLACED UPON COMPETITORS IN A RACE OR OTHER CONTEST TO EQUALIZE THEIR CHANCES OF WINNING. WELL, WE THINK HANDICAPS ARE A GREAT IDEA, AND THEIR POTENTIALS HAVE HARDLY BEEN TAPPED. JOIN US NOW AS MAD DEVISES SOME . . .

HANDICAPS IN OTHER FIELDS

ARTIST: HARRY NORTH, ESQ.   IDEA: ADAM GARST   WRITER: LARRY SIEGEL

Every Saturday night, the leading club in the NBA would have to field an all white basketball team.

Clint Eastwood would have to deliver all his lines in his next movie with his mouth open.

Hollywood's most successful studio would be forced to go an entire year without making a "Disaster Movie."

The current Wrestling Champion would have to perform his next match without a script.

Elton John would have to give concerts in a Brooks Brothers suit and contact lenses.

Every Mafiosa Don would be forced to operate one month a year without his two best weapons—his Judge and his Police Captain.

The week's leading Rock group would have to perform an entire number without swaying, snapping fingers or using the word "baby."

Muhammad Ali would have to fight his next Championship bout with his mouth gagged.

It's ROMANCE when you're beguiled by an introduction to a MAD article like this one. It's LOVE when you have the blind faith to read on in the vain hope that you're going to run into something funny. And it's a RELATIONSHIP when you get through the entire article and you realize you've been duped again, but you still keep buying the magazine for some strange reason you can't explain. All of which is our way of introducing

It's ROMANCE...

... when you think her
hyena laugh is cute.

It's LOVE...

... when you accept that her hyena
laugh is part of her personality.

MAD'S "ROMANCE-LOVE-RELATIONSHIP" BOOK

ARTIST: PAUL COKER, JR.
WRITER: FRANK JACOBS

It's a RELATIONSHIP . . .

. . . when you realize there's more
to life than just having laughs.

It's ROMANCE...

... when you take him
to meet your friends.

It's LOVE...

... when you take him
to meet your family.

It's a RELATIONSHIP...

... when you take him
to meet your analyst.

It's ROMANCE...

...when you get excited watching his favorite football team on TV.

It's LOVE...

...when you become as excited a fan as he is.

It's a RELATIONSHIP...

...when you realize that's the high point of your excitement together.

It's ROMANCE...

. . . when you lie to
him about your age.

It's LOVE...

. . . when you lie to him about your
age, and he knows you're lying.

It's a RELATIONSHIP...

. . . when you tell him your real age,
and he wishes you were still lying.

It's ROMANCE...

... when you plan your
week-end around her.

It's LOVE...

... when you plan your
lifetime around her.

It's a RELATIONSHIP...

... when you plan your
income tax return around her.

It's ROMANCE...

. . . when he loves
the way you dress.

It's LOVE...

. . . when he helps you pick
out clothes at the store.

It's a RELATIONSHIP...

. . . when he asks you if
sometimes he can wear them.

It's ROMANCE...

... when you surprise him
with a birthday gift.

It's LOVE...

... when you don't mind
that he doesn't like it.

It's a RELATIONSHIP...

... when he asks
you to return it.

It's ROMANCE...

... when it makes no difference
where you spend your vacation.

It's LOVE...

... when you want to go camping
and she wants to go sailing ...
and you give in and go sailing.

It's a RELATIONSHIP...

...when you want to go camping, and
she wants to go sailing ... and you
go camping ... and she goes sailing.

It's ROMANCE...

... when she thinks you're the
greatest lover in the world.

It's LOVE...

... when she accepts the fact that
even the greatest lover in the
world can't perform occasionally.

It's a RELATIONSHIP...

... when you spend a
lot of time reminiscing.

ONE MORNING IN A DRUG STORE

New York has been called "Fun City"...but not by anyone who lives there! That's propaganda for the tourists. However, someone must have been taken in by all that nonsense, because there's actually a TV Show that's about New York City Policemen who have a wild, fun time each week. The leader of this gang of chuckleheads is named Barney Miller. But after seeing several episodes of this totally unbelievable series, we prefer to call it:

BLARNEY MILLER

ARTIST: ANGELO TORRES   WRITER: STAN HART

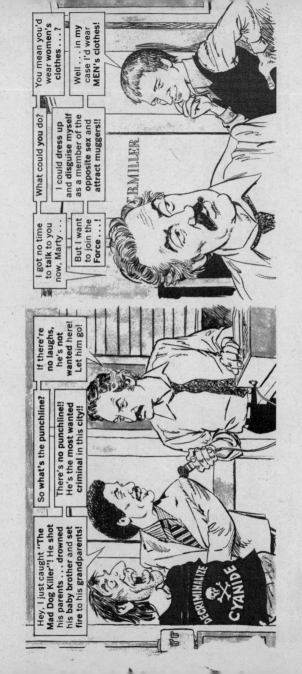

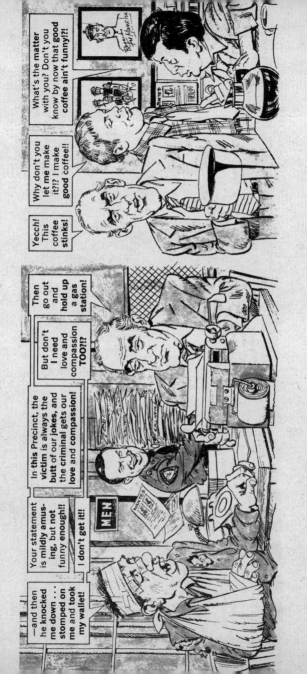